cat

կատու
katow

rabbit

Ճագար

čagar

dog

หมา
šown

chick

ᦵᦀᦶᦺ

čowt

duck
բադ
bad

sheep

ոչխար
oč̌ xar

goat

ажы
ауc

pig

hunq
xoz

donkey

ապանակ
avanak

horse

ḁḥ
ji

cow

կով
kov

mouse

մուկ
mowk

bat

č łjik

bee

մեղու

meɫow

spider

սարդ
sard

fox

 աղվես
aɫves

deer

եղնիկ

ełnik

squirrel

սկյուռ
skyow

hedgehog

ոզնի
ozni

owl

ᗷ0M
bow

frog

գորտ
gort

snake
oð
ōj

racoon

ӌпꭒрӌ
ǰrarǰ

parrot

թութակ

t owt ak

toucan

տուկան
towkan

alligator

ալիգատոր
aligator

sea turtle

ծովային կրիա

covayin kria

flamingo

ֆլամինգո
flamingo

penguin

պինգվին
pingvin

crab

խեցգետին
xec getin

jellyfish

մեդուզա
medowza

seal

փոկ

p ok

shark

Շնաձուկ
šnajowk

whale

लेॻ
ket

orca

խոյադելֆին

ōrka

starfish
ծոֆասող
cōvastł

rhinoceros

ոնգեռջյուր

ngełjyowr

panda

պանդա
panda

monkey

կապիկ
kapik

lion

a yowc

tiger

վագր
vagr

elephant

փիղ
p ił

www.ingramcontent.com/pod-product-compliance
Lightning Source LLC
LaVergne TN
LVHW071626180726
843512LV00002B/254